GOD'S PROSPERITY PROMISES

Putting Subconscious Faith to Work

Daniel R. Williamson

GOD'S PROSPERITY PROMISES
Copyright ©2017, 2018, 2019, 2020, 2021
Daniel R. Williamson

*All Scriptures are taken from the
King James Version of the Bible.*

Revision of *God's Prosperity Promises*

Book Cover Photo
*North Side of Mt. Shasta in California
Taken by Kathleen Williamson*

Table of Contents

Dedication

In our lives some stars shine brighter than others. In my life my wife Kathleen is just such a star. When I was lost in the cold night of this world, her brightness and warmth led me safely home. Only God knows how many selfless hours she spent typing and editing this and my other books. They would not have been completed without her. Thank you, Kathleen, for your generous support and for sticking in there with me. Thank you, God, for my very own North Star.

I Promise You

I cannot describe the joy you will receive when you pray, believe, and receive a need or want from God. After you receive what you have believed God's written promises for, your faith in God and His written Word will become even stronger.

By the time you have reached the end of this book, you will have received everything a Bible-knowledgeable Christian needs to know in order to receive from God's written promises.

I promise you that if you will put the things you will learn in this book into practice in your life, success will follow.

Introduction

This book is all about empowering Christians by providing them with the understandings needed to successfully receive from the promises of God written in His Word. Christians know God's written promises found in the Bible, but few have a complete picture of what they mean and how they all fit together.

Receiving by believing and trusting God's promises found in the Bible is like a puzzle, which few Christians have put together on a regular basis. I think everyone of us has taken one or two Bible verses and confessed them repeatedly over circumstances in our lives and hoped God would grant our petitions. If your results were like mine, they were mixed at best. My brothers and sisters in Christ, we can do better, much better.

Let me make something perfectly clear. God's written promises are promises from God, where we can make use of His power to meet our needs and desires. If you don't feel that the power of God is available to you, my friend, you have not put all the pieces of the puzzle together. This book was written to help you put all the pieces of the prosperity puzzle together so you too can have the power of God that is available to you in your life.

I want to give you a heads up or a little warning though. There will be resistance to your learning and putting into practice the information found in this book. I'm not speaking of your preacher, church friends, relatives, or close friends. I'm speaking of your own subconscious mind.

We are humans. Humans have subconscious minds. Subconscious minds label all new information as false, or at least suspicious, if it doesn't agree with what they already believe.

Only those readers who want to know the truth more than their subconscious minds want to protect what they already believe to be the truth will receive the truth.

Personally, I was offended when I learned for the first time that my subconscious mind was influencing what I believed. Like many of the readers of this book, I prided myself in being a person who made logical decisions on what I believed. Once I learned the truth concerning how I believed, I could not put that genie back into the bottle. The good news though is that I'm learning how to deal with my subconscious mind to my advantage, and you can do the same.

My secrets will soon be your secrets.

Accessing Prosperity

This book is for those Christians who have a lot of knowledge about prosperity from God but have precious few good results. Does this sound like you? I know it sounds like my wife and me for most of our adult lives.

You may be a doer of God's written Word, not just a hearer only. It could be that even after giving to God cheerfully, imaging being successful, rebuking Satan, and even confessing the Word of God on a regular basis, you still aren't receiving much success from believing in God's promises. You really don't know what you are doing wrong but you suspect it might have to do with doubting. I also suspect doubt in your heart might be one source that is causing your difficulties, but there could also be other reasons.

My wife and I also know the disappointment, the confusion, and the shame of failure when we were not able to receive from the promises of God. But we also have experienced the joy of knowing that God and His written Word can be trusted.

Because of my wife's and my walk with the Lord, I am absolutely confident that by the time you have finished this book, you will have received all the understanding you need to successfully pursue your endeavor to receive from believing in God's written promises.

Do you dream of helping your brothers and sisters in Christ to have better lives and become closer to God? Maybe *God's Prosperity Promises* is just what you have been looking for.

Why You Should Believe God for Things

Believing God for things is not easy. There is a lot to learn, a lot to do, and a lot not to do when it comes to believing God for things.

You should believe God for things because God wants you to ask and believe Him for things. He knows it is a great way to learn about Him and the power of His Word. Doing all things associated with believing is a real soul builder.

Beloved, I wish above all things that thou mayest prosper and be in health, even as thy soul prospereth.
III John 1:2

Notice in the previous Bible verse what the last five words say: "even as thy soul prospereth." If you are wise, you will never forget that prosperity of your soul is the most important prosperity there is.

For what shall it profit a man, if he shall gain the whole world, and lose his own soul?
Mark 8:36

You never have to worry about asking God for too much, as you can see by the first Bible verse above (III John 1:2). He is not going to give you more than your soul can handle.

Experience creates confidence, and when it comes to believing, every one of us can use all the confidence we can get. For that reason, my advice to believers is not to overlook believing God for small things. It is much easier to remove a mole hill than it is to remove a mountain. In other words, it is easier to start believing for small things because when you receive them, probably more quickly, it will build your confidence for believing God for bigger things.

But while you wait to receive, you need to be content with the things you already have.

> Let your conversation be without covetousness; and be content with such things as ye have: for he hath said, I will never leave thee, nor forsake thee.
> Hebrews 13:5

God also wants His people to prosper so they will have the means to help others. There have been many souls won when Christians did good deeds for others because they had the means to help them.

You may want to consider this: When non-Christians see Christians prosper in life, it gives them hope and a good reason to check out God and His written Word.

The last reason I will mention why God desires for His children to learn to receive from His written promises is the most important one to consider. Christians need to learn how to function in heaven as spirit beings.

Learning to receive from God's written promises is all about learning to walk by faith, not by sight. Walking by faith is the way we will function in heaven. If we have not learned to walk by faith before we go to heaven, we will miss out on a lot of wonderful blessings.

Earth is our classroom. We should make good use of our time here. Personally, I'm trying to get an "A" in walking by faith.

In the next chapter, we are going to look at a few things believers sometimes fail to completely understand. Then after that we will move on to more challenging concepts.

Planting in Your Own Field

In retrospect, I should have understood the following principal, but I did not fully comprehend it for many years.

We must plant seed in our own fields. Giving tithes and offerings to God through our local churches is both our duty and our good pleasure but we cannot stop there and expect to receive our dreams, desires, and needs. For no farmer plants all his seed money in his local church and then expects to receive a harvest without planting seed in his own field.

For far too many years, I gave my offerings to my local church and other worthy ministries. After watering my field with prayers and confessions of my faith, my fields produced weeds or very little in the way of a harvest. I thank God that He finally opened my eyes to the truth in His Word about seeding my own fields. If your harvests are small, please consider seeding your own fields.

I recommend for every dollar you give to God that you also give at least a dollar to yourself for seed to plant in your own fields or investments of your choosing. Planting the right kind of seed is also necessary. If a farmer wanted to harvest corn, he would not plant wheat seed. For example, if you believe God is going to give you a new home, you might want to donate time and money to an organization like Habitat for America as a spiritual seed. Also, you might want to start a savings account at your local bank that makes housing loans and use that as a physical seed.

Don't forget to tell God what you want your seed to produce. It may seem like a small matter, but it is important.

I have a pet peeve. Some preachers preach week after week about sowing seed by giving offerings to the Lord. Seldom do I hear them preach about the need of preparing fields to receive God's spiritual blessings. By the way, farmers usually have several fields. Maybe believers should also have several fields.

Physical prosperity fields are anything with the potential of being financially rewarding in the future. A few examples of fields that God could bless are jobs with higher earning potential, education, investments, new businesses, certain hobbies, professional occupations, and trade careers.

I grew up in a farming community in North Central Ohio. Most of my neighbors and friends were farmers. Without exception, they loved and cared for their fields like they were their children.

I am sure you too will enjoy planting spiritual and physical seed in your fields. Watering your fields by confessing your faith in the Word of God should be more of a pleasure than a chore.

Placing Faith in Your Heart

To receive the promises of God, you must speak faith-filled words from your heart over your circumstances. Before you can speak faith-filled words from your heart, you must first place them in your heart. The question is how do you get the promises of God into your heart?

> So then faith cometh by hearing, and hearing by the word of God.
>
> Romans 10:17

I suggest to you that hearing must take place in both your physical ears and in the spiritual ears of your heart for God's promises to become faith in your heart.

Sound waves vibrating will cause your physical ears to hear, but not the spiritual ears in your heart. For your spiritual heart to hear words, the words must be believed. The stronger you believe God's promises and the greater the emotions that are attached to what you believe God is going to do for you, the easier it is for your heart to hear and place faith in those words.

Placing words of faith in your heart will program your subconscious mind for success. Winning in life will become natural.

Attaching emotions to what you believe does not come easily for many of us. If you have not personally witnessed the fulfillment of the promises of God, it can be very hard to believe it could happen in your life. You cannot overestimate the importance of emotions in the process of believing.

Imaging your victories to create emotion before you speak the Word of God to your heart can help a lot, but sometimes you need even more help. Doing what you know God wants you to do in your life can produce the spiritual emotions needed to place the Word of God in your heart. Remember what Jesus said at the well with the Samaritan woman?

> But he said unto them, I have meat to eat that ye know not of.
>
> John 4:32

By doing the will of God before arriving at the well and then at the well, Jesus received spiritual energy (meat) that He needed in order to do what God wanted Him to do in the next village that he was going to.

You can have confidence in God when you do His will because your heart will not condemn you for not doing His will. There is real power in obeying God, and when you do, you will feel better about yourself. Feeling good about yourself is a powerful tool to help you receive from God's promises.

> [21] Beloved, if our heart condemn us not, then have we confidence toward God.
> [22] And whatsoever we ask, we receive of him, because we keep his commandments, and do those things that are pleasing in his sight.
>
> I John 3:21-22

While on the subject of creating emotions to add to what you are believing to receive from the promises of God, let me add one more thing. God does not need offerings. He has everything He needs or wants. God receives offerings to help you create the positive emotions needed to place His Word in your heart as faith; so if you feel good about giving God an offering, by all means do so with joy, not out of necessity.

Before starting any project that requires help from God to accomplish, I give an offering to God to make my heart feel good. I do it cheerfully, not because I have to.

Giving offerings to God is optional for Christians, but paying tithes is not optional. When you don't pay tithes, it is stealing from God.

Satan Comes Immediately

And these are they by the way side, where the word is sown; but when they have heard, Satan cometh immediately, and taketh away the word that was sown in their hearts.

Mark 4:15

No one has to tell me Satan comes immediately. There was a time in my life where I was actually afraid to pray and ask God for something. If you think about it, there were probably times in your life also that after you prayed to God for something, Satan showed up on the run. Am I correct?

It is written that God is not a respecter of persons.

Then Peter opened his mouth, and said, Of a truth I perceive that God is no respecter of persons:

Acts 10:34

If God doesn't determine who receives from the promises of God, then who is the one who makes the determination?

I can only see one reasonable answer to the previous question. It is you who determines if you are successful or not in receiving what you believe to receive from God. It is you who must pass Satan's test by not letting Satan steal your peace or faith in God's written Word.

Personally, I love the idea that it is up to me if I receive from God's written Word or not. I'm motivated by my responsibility.

> Peace I leave with you, my peace I give unto you: not as the world giveth, give I unto you. Let not your heart be troubled, neither let it be afraid.
>
> John 14:27

After praying to God to receive what you desire, Satan will come to test your faith and patience as a believer. Satan must come or your faith will not have an opportunity to become stronger.

In order to pass Satan's test, you must choose to believe the Word of God over what you see in the physical world. You must trust the Word of God and confess that God's Word is the truth. Finally, you must rebuke Satan by casting him and his mountain (which is his authority) into the sea by using the name of Jesus. The name of Jesus is the power and authority that God gave to Jesus, which He gave to His believers.

> Behold, I give unto you power to tread on serpents and scorpions, and over all the power of the enemy: and nothing shall by any means hurt you.
>
> Luke 10:19

Be aware that tribulations will come into your life.

> These things I have spoken unto you, that in me ye might have peace. In the world ye shall have tribulation: but be of good cheer; I have overcome the world.
>
> John 16:33

Trusting, obeying, and confessing God's Word in the name of Jesus will defeat Satan and cause your faith to have the power to change your circumstances in order to give you victories.

Satan is the author and finisher of your doubt. Defeating Satan prevents doubt from entering into your heart and mind. Always be ready to rebuke the father of lies.

If You Have Doubt

²³ For verily I say unto you, That whosoever shall say unto this mountain, Be thou removed, and be thou cast into the sea; and shall not doubt in his heart, but shall believe that those things which he saith shall come to pass; he shall have whatsoever he saith.
²⁴ Therefore I say unto you, What things soever ye desire, when ye pray, believe that ye receive *them*, and ye shall have *them*.

Mark 11:23-24

There was a time in my life when I began to think God would prosper almost anyone but me. Then for some reason (it must have been the Holy Spirit prompting me), I decided to read and meditate on the above Bible verses daily. I am so glad that I did.

The verses from Mark 11:23-24 turned my understanding about prosperity around. Without a doubt they can do the same thing for anyone. Let's take a look at some of the valuable lessons to be gained from studying them.

It is written in verse 23 ". . . say unto this mountain, Be thou removed, and be thou cast in to the sea." "This mountain" is any spiritual thing that is trying to prevent you from receiving the promises of God. In the context of this book, the mountain we need to deal with is fear and doubt.

God has given you His great two-edged sword, which is His Word. To be effective you must swing the sword in two directions. The first thing you need to do is to put fear in the heart of your enemy. Demanding your enemy to be removed from you and be cast into the sea in the name of Jesus will accomplish that task.

What a lot of believers don't realize is that when you move this mountain (any opposing spiritual thing, or in this case the fear of lack) and cast it into the sea, you must believe that the power of the name of Jesus really does remove that spirit and cast it into the sea.

The sea mentioned in Mark 11:23 is not one of our physical oceans. This sea is a spiritual place for spirit beings. It was created when God gave the name Seas to gathered waters. Spirit realms were created whenever God named one of His creations.

Satan is the god of this world (II Corinthians 4:4), so you must bind him with the Word of God before you receive God's promises. In my opinion, the above is one of the most overlooked problems Christian believers have concerning receiving God's promises.

In verse 23 it is also written ". . .but shall believe that those things which he saith shall come to pass; he shall have whatsoever he saith." We all know this Word of God as the other side of the two-edged sword which builds faith in the hearts of believers. This is the faith needed to keep doubt out of your heart and to bring forth the promises of God.

You are not to wait until you receive something in the physical world before you believe that you have received the thing you prayed for. You must believe God placed in your heart what you prayed for as a spiritual blessing at the very time you prayed.

That means God is not going to give it to you in the future but that He has already given it to you now in the spiritual world. It's what you do and say that determines when, where, how, and if God's blessings to you will manifest in the physical world or not. Be grateful for the responsibility and control God has given to you.

When it comes to the written promises of God, you need to walk by faith, not by sight.

> (For we walk by faith, not by sight:)
> II Corinthians 5:7

Walking by faith in this case means that every time you think about what you believe God is going to do for you, you start your thoughts with the faith fact that God has already given you what you prayed for as a spiritual blessing. Those who have learned how to walk by faith are much more successful in receiving from God's promises than those who have not.

When it comes to doubt in your heart, an ounce of prevention is more valuable than a pound of cure. It is far better for you to keep doubt out of your heart than to have to spend the time and effort to get it out.

Do the following often to build faith and to fight doubt. Visualize that you have received in the physical what you believe God is going to do for you. Try to feel the joy you would have if it really was true. Now praise God and confess out loud that God has given you what you are believing Him for, which is true because He has already placed it in your heart as a spiritual blessing.

The greater your trust in God's written Word is, the easier it is to generate joy when you are imaging successfully receiving from God's promises. Therefore, if it is hard for you to create joy, chances are you lack faith that God really does give you spiritual blessings at the time you pray.

Let's take another look at what is said in God's written Word.

> Therefore I say unto you, What things soever ye desire, when ye pray, believe that ye receive them, and ye shall have them.
>
> Mark 11:24

You are to "believe that ye receive them" as spiritual blessings at the time you prayed. You are also to believe "ye shall have them" later in the physical world. The importance of this understanding cannot be overestimated.

The previous exercise is a real doubt fighter and faith builder, so do it often. It will become easier and more natural with practice.

Faith's Biggest Secret

For most of my Christian life, I was concerned with increasing my faith. I thought my lack of faith was the reason for my poor results in receiving from God, but I was wrong. Faith is important but we only need faith of a mustard seed to get most things done.

> And Jesus said unto them, Because of your unbelief: for verily I say unto you, If ye have faith as a grain of mustard seed, ye shall say unto this mountain, Remove hence to yonder place; and it shall remove; and nothing shall be impossible unto you.
>
> Matthew 17:20

Lack of regular faith was not my problem. My problem was the lack of faith that had been tested by fire.

> That the trial of your faith, being much more precious than of gold that perisheth, though it be tried with fire, might be found unto praise and honour and glory at the appearing of Jesus Christ:
>
> I Peter 1:7

To have power, faith must first be tested by trials and temptations. To pass a faith test, you must believe the Word of God, obey the Word of God, and confess what the written Word of God says about your circumstances instead of what you see, hear, and feel in the physical world. Also, you must rebuke Satan by confessing God's written Word and then casting Satan out of your life.

Remember how Jesus returned with the power of God after His faith was tested in the wilderness?

> [13] And when the devil had ended all the temptation, he departed from him for a season.
> [14] And Jesus returned in the power of the Spirit into Galilee: and there went out a fame of him through all the region round about.
>
> Luke 4:13-14

Faith that has not been tested is still a good thing to have because it will help its owner do the righteous thing when tested. Whereas faith that has been tested by fire has the power of God to change your circumstances like only God could do.

Don't Waste Your Losses

If you belong to a Bible-believing faith church, chances are that many times you have heard much of the material we've covered so far. What you probably have not heard is that most Christians are throwing away valuable losses and defeats.

Both losses and defeats will cause your faith to become powerful if you confess and obey the written Word of God instead of confessing your physical circumstances at the time they occur. You cannot lose when you have a loss or a defeat if you obey and confess the Word of God instead of what Satan wants you to say and do, because your faith will become like gold and will increase in power. Waiting for victories to build your faith can take a long time, so why should you wait? Don't waste your losses and defeats.

> That the trial of your faith, being much more precious than of gold that perisheth, though it be tried with fire, might be found unto praise and honour and glory at the appearing of Jesus Christ:
>
> I Peter 1:7

We all know the story of Job who suffered unbelievable losses but kept his faith in God. Job knew God would repay him for all that he suffered.

> But he knoweth the way that I take: when he hath tried me, I shall come forth as gold.
>
> Job 23:10

Because Job kept his faithfulness, God blessed him and made him twice as powerful as he was at the beginning of all his trials and tribulations.

> And the LORD turned the captivity of Job, when he prayed for his friends: also the LORD gave Job twice as much as he had before.
>
> Job 42:10

Joseph is another powerful story of someone who didn't let Satan steal his peace and his faith in God. After suffering unjustly but still doing what was right in God's eyes, he was given the power of second ruler of Egypt.

Every one of us is going to have some losses and defeats in our lives. We might as well do the right thing and receive power from them. Don't let negative emotions control your future. Release them, and they will release you.

Don't waste your time thinking about the lost opportunities of building your faith from past losses or defeats. That would only make things worse.

Since you know losses and defeats will be coming in your life, do the wise thing and mentally prepare yourself to do the righteous thing when they do occur.

By the way, if you do the righteous thing after experiencing a loss or defeat, it will help take some of the sting out of the event. I am speaking from experience. In the past, I have at different times been both unrighteous and righteous after suffering losses or defeats. Righteous is a better way to go.

Another Prosperity Blessing

Before writing the following words, I stood in front of my mirror and thought about all of you, about me, and about prosperity. I imagined all of you being a lot like me.

I imagined that all of you absolutely believe God's written Word and know that God has pleasure in the prosperity of His servants. Even so, you still have doubts about receiving God's promises, not because of God but because of what may be lacking in you.

> Let them shout for joy, and be glad, that favour my righteous cause: yea, let them say continually, Let the LORD be magnified, which hath pleasure in the prosperity of his servant.
>
> Psalm 35:27

You know God wants to prosper you but only to the point where your soul can handle it.

> Beloved, I wish above all things that thou mayest prosper and be in health, even as thy soul prospereth.
>
> III John 1:2

You have probably come a long way since you made Jesus your Lord and Savior; but, to be honest, when you look into the mirror, you probably cannot help but think that you still have a long, long way to go.

You know God loves you but you also know, as previously stated, He is only going to allow you to prosper to the point where your soul can handle it. The question is how are you going to build up your soul to the point where you can receive the amazing things that you believe God will give you?

Knowing and doing all the things covered in this book will help, but you know doing so could take a long time. You also know you are not to have any doubt in your heart, but it's hard when you think of the limited time you have on Planet Earth.

I have great news, friends. God has placed instructions in His written Word on how you can use His laws to start prospering and how you can build up your faith, even if your soul is not as healthy as you would like it to be.

> Be not deceived; God is not mocked: for what-
> soever a man soweth, that shall he also reap.
> > Galatians 6:7

When understood and used correctly, the spiritual "law of seedtime and harvest" is a magnificent and powerful tool for the completion of your dreams, wants, and needs.

> While the earth remaineth, seedtime and harvest,
> and cold and heat, and summer and winter, and day
> and night shall not cease.
> > Genesis 8:22

It is well-understood that the law of seedtime and harvest is a karma-like law to return good or bad upon people depending on what seeds they sowed, but there is much more to it than most people know. It is also a great mechanism to help prosper believers.

The law of seedtime and harvest works like this: Whatever you want to receive, you need to sow it as seed. Let's say you need financial prosperity. You therefore need to sow financial prosperity. You should look for ways and opportunities to help others to gain financial prosperity. Helping others to help themselves is a wonderful way to help you gain your own prosperity in those fields.

I encourage you to look at the things you are believing God for and search for opportunities to plant seed in those fields. Seed for the law of seedtime and harvest does not have to be money. Spiritual seed can be anything that helps others become successful. Simple things like babysitting when a neighbor is attending night school, giving a co-worker a ride to work, or telling someone about a job opening at your work could all be excellent spiritual seed.

Physical seed can be anything to help yourself in the future, such as training, getting education, or volunteering in the field you want to work in. The time and effort spent in hobbies with the potential of making money in the future, such as quilting, painting, writing, or metal detecting, could also be used as physical seed.

Planting spiritual and physical seed are probably the most important things anyone who wants prosperity can do to succeed. Planting seed is the right thing to do. It will make you feel good about yourself and your future.

I suggest that you take note of successful people and figure out what kind of fields they are planting their seeds in. Ask yourself if any of those fields would be a good suit for you. Do any of them motivate you? Sooner or later you will probably find just what you are looking for.

There is a very important difference between the law that many people call karma and the law of seedtime and harvest. The law called karma works on a one-to-one basis. A deed done to others will return back to the sender. The law of seedtime and harvest is a blessing God gave mankind after the Great Flood to meet the needs and wants of mankind (Genesis 8:20-22). Seeds sown can multiply to create a bountiful harvest. Some seeds can produce 60, some 80, and some 100 fold.

> [20] And Noah builded an altar unto the LORD; and took of every clean beast, and of every clean fowl, and offered burnt offerings on the altar.
> [21] And the LORD smelled a sweet savour; and the LORD said in his heart, I will not again curse the ground any more for man's sake; for the imagination of man's heart is evil from his youth; neither will I again smite any more every thing living, as I have done.
> [22] While the earth remaineth, seedtime and harvest, and cold and heat, and summer and winter, and day and night shall not cease.
>
> Genesis 8:20-22

I have heard many times that God helps those who help themselves. For many years I would pray and ask God for something, then I would go sit on my couch and believe God would provide. It did not occur to me that I had to help myself by planting a field in order to receive the blessings God had already given to me in the spiritual world.

Why Winners Win and Losers Lose

I am a Cleveland Browns fan. I was born and raised in Wayne County, Ohio, which is about fifty miles south of Cleveland. Like Browns fans everywhere, my heart was broken on many Sunday afternoons when my team lost. To the east of where I lived most people liked the Pittsburg Steelers. Pittsburg Steelers' fans have many sweet memories of their team being victorious on Sunday afternoons, so when all things are equal, why do winners win and losers lose?

It is my belief that winners do two things different from losers. Winners expect to win and don't fear losing, even if they are behind in the game. Losers hope to win and fear losing, even if they are ahead in the game. Those who win repeatedly draw from the joy of previous wins to give them the ability to expect to win. Those who lose repeatedly draw from the pain of previous losses to create the fear of losing.

The road to riches for the Pittsburg Steelers started many years ago with one unforgettable miracle-like play in Oakland, California. In my opinion, that one play gave the Steelers many victories over the years. Unfortunately for my team, the Cleveland Browns, both the Denver Broncos and the Oakland Raiders have provided them with good reasons to fear losing. If the Browns and their fans are ever going to become winners again, they must find a way to stop thinking about past heartbreaks and find a way to expect to win at all times, no matter what the score happens to be.

The same can be said about all of us. If you are ever going to become a winner in different aspects of your life, you too must use the joy of previous victories in order to expect to win, and you must prevent the pain of previous losses from causing you to fear defeat.

God has provided a way for you to become a winner, even if you lack the experience of winning in the past. God has given you the ability to imagine victories. Your subconscious mind cannot tell the difference from an imagined experience and a real past experience, which allows you to have real emotion. Real emotion is a key element in the ability to believe, because strong emotions allow you to place what you believe in your heart.

Is there an aspect of your life where you wish you had victory? If so, do the following. When you pray to God for something, believe you have received what you prayed for at that time. Sow spiritual and physical seed. Repeatedly visualize receiving the thing you prayed for, and try your best to feel as if you have already received it. Confess your faith in the Word of God, and thank God for His faithfulness. Expect to receive what you prayed for, and don't doubt or fear that you are not going to receive it.

When it comes to receiving the promises of God found in the Bible, believing is easy, but not doubting is hard. Jesus said if you have the faith of a mustard seed and do not doubt in your heart, you could speak to the mountain and it would be cast into the sea (Matthew 17:20).

Not doubting is hard, but with practice it does become much easier. Never think about what you would do if you didn't receive what you believe God is going to provide for you, and try not to have a deadline of when you must receive it. Keep your eyes on the prize, not on anything that might cause you to doubt.

Winning or losing is in your own hands, because God is not a respecter of persons. He has created each of us with the ability to win or to lose. In the game of life there will be times when defeat seems likely, but winners refuse to let go of their vision of victory until the last whistle blows.

Know for certain in your faith walk with God that Satan will show up to challenge your faith. Be ready for him, and do what you know you should do at that time rather than what you feel like doing.

On the way to a championship, it is hard to win every game. If you experience a loss or defeat in life, don't waste your time thinking about it over and over. Confess that God has made you a winner and not a loser. Then start visualizing winning your next game. Your faith will become more valuable than gold as it receives power from God.

Coaches, bosses, and parents: remind your team of the joy of previous wins, not the pain of previous losses. Help them become winners by programming their subconscious minds for winning.

Act Like a Winner

Actors and actresses sometimes adopt the personal traits of the people they are portraying. The written Word of God says we are victorious, so let's act the part.

> But thanks be to God, which giveth us the victory through our Lord Jesus Christ.
>
> I Corinthians 15:57

> For whatsoever is born of God overcometh the world: and this is the victory that overcometh the world, even our faith.
>
> I John 5:4

Envision yourself as a winner doing things that you want to accomplish. You need to feel, act, and speak like you have already won. In other words, "Be a winner." Keeping the image in your mind, the feeling in your heart, and the confessing of faith in your mouth will cause you to become the winner that the Word of God says you are.

If you are waiting to win before you feel like you are a winner, you might have a very long wait. Winners win because they are already winners in their hearts. God has given you an imagination, so be a winner and use it.

Acting like a winner has nothing to do with fooling others. Acting like a winner is about painting a picture in your mind to show your own subconscious mind how it should conduct its day-to-day activities and is a necessary step in building faith up in your heart.

The true purpose of acting like a winner is to allow yourself to feel like a winner in your heart. If you feel like a winner in your heart, the supernatural power of God will make it so in the physical world.

We walk by faith, not by sight. Christians like us have heard II Corinthians 5:7 more times than we could count, but do we truly understand its meaning? I wonder.

(For we walk by faith, not by sight:)
II Corinthians 5:7

In this Bible verse, we are told we need to live by the Word of God, not by what we see, hear, feel, or touch in the physical world. As far as believing God's prosperity promises, please allow me to tell you what I think this verse means.

When you stand on God's written promises found in the Bible, you are to believe that you receive it as a spiritual blessing at the time you prayed, if it was according to God's written Word. His written Word is His will.

You are to visualize that you have already received what you prayed for, feel the joy as if you really have received it in the physical, and thank God that He answered your prayers. As you can see, it is not easy walking by faith, but it is a faith test that we all must pass.

Some of my favorite prosperity preachers who now have large successful ministries started off preaching with actual holes in their shoes. They walked by faith, not by sight. They put their trust in God's written Word, not thinking about the holes in the bottom of their shoes. They believed in their success because they knew God had already given them prosperity as a spiritual blessing.

If you are going to be successful in receiving from God's prosperity promises, you must do what those prosperity preachers did. You must walk by faith keeping your eyes on the spiritual blessings God gave you and not on what you have or don't have yet in the physical world.

All those who attempt to walk by faith or believe in God's prosperity promises will be tempted by Satan. He will say things like "Open your eyes, you are being deceived and are trying to deceive others."

Be ready at all times to cast Satan down and replace negative thoughts with God's written Word.

Walking by faith is acting like a winner to feel like a winner. Feeling like a winner is a necessary step to becoming a winner.

Subconscious Faith

Having faith is the expectation that something good will happen. To fear is the opposite. It is the expectation that something bad will happen.

The faith and fear that you are aware of are conscious faith and conscious fear. They influence all aspects of your life, including what you think, feel, say, and do.

Controlling your thoughts is the key to controlling your reactions to lives' many circumstances. There are many good books written on managing your thoughts. I highly recommend *Battlefield of the Mind* by Joyce Meyer.

On a deeper level, within your spiritual heart, subconscious faith and subconscious fear are in the very presence of the power of God; whereas, faith and fear on the conscious level of your awareness greatly influences your reactions to lives' many circumstances.

Subconscious faith, subconscious fear, and doubt influence your life in two different ways. First, they whisper their opinions to your conscious thoughts to softly guide your thoughts and your actions in your day-to-day life. Secondly, subconscious faith, subconscious fear, and doubt are in the presence of the power of God. They are what God looks at to determine when or if you will receive what you believe God is going to do for you. The power of God supernaturally changes the circumstances in your life to match what you believe subconsciously in your heart, for good or for bad.

Jesus said unto him, If thou canst believe, all
things are possible to him that believeth.

Mark 9:23

For as he thinketh in his heart, so is he:. . .

Proverbs 23:7

Do you believe that God will give you a miracle? If so, you
need to get what you believe God has given to you down into
your heart as subconscious faith.

God has given you the ability and the responsibility of
influencing what happens in your life by speaking faith-filled
words from your spiritual heart.

20 A man's belly shall be satisfied with the fruit of
his mouth; and with the increase of his lips shall he
be filled.
21 Death and life are in the power of the tongue:
and they that love it shall eat the fruit thereof.

Proverbs 18:20-21

This God-given power is not magic. It was given to man by
God for the purpose of evolving us mentally and spiritually to
prepare us for heaven as well as to give us better lives here on
the physical earth.

Conscious faith and subconscious faith are wonderful things
to have, but if you have subconscious fear, subconscious fear
will almost always win. I'm sure that every one of you has
believed the Word of God for something and then has been sadly
disappointed when it didn't happen. You probably usually say
you didn't have enough faith or it was not God's will to receive
what you wanted. It really could have been your lack of faith or

44

that it wasn't God's will, but it is much more likely that it was because in addition to your faith, you also had subconscious fear and doubt.

You should never worry if God will grant your prayer request. If it is according to His written Word, it is according to His will, and God will always grant your request. If your faith's strength level is high enough, you will receive it.

If ye abide in me, and my words abide in you, ye
shall ask what ye will, and it shall be done unto you.
John 15:7

For all the promises of God in him are yea, and
in him Amen, unto the glory of God by us.
II Corinthians 1:20

The thing you should be concerned with is creating spiritual faith in your heart, because that is where God's supernatural power to grant your request in the physical world is located.

Since you are reading this book, I know you want to be prosperous. If you have wanted to be prosperous for a long time, there is no doubt that wanting to be prosperous is in your subconscious mind or spiritual heart.

As far as your subconscious mind or spiritual heart is concerned, wanting to be prosperous is more than an emotion. Your wanting to be prosperous is the absolute truth about yourself, and it will always do everything it can to always protect it as truth. It will always cause you to want to be prosperous by preventing you from becoming prosperous.

For you to become prosperous in the physical world, you must replace "wanting to be prosperous" with "you are prosperous" in your spiritual heart. If you can convince your spiritual heart that you are prosperous, the supernatural power of God will work to make it true in the physical world. Also, your subconscious mind will influence your conscious mind to do what needs to be done in order for you to receive prosperity.

Replacing long-held understandings and beliefs can be very difficult, but spiritual growth is well worth all the effort. Someday each and every one of us will hear Jesus knocking on our doors. Let Him find us hard at work toward our spiritual maturity.

If you desire the power of God in your life, you must place subconscious faith in your spiritual heart and keep subconscious fear and doubt out. So how do you place faith in your heart and keep fear and doubt out? The answer is "emotion." Adding as much positive emotion as you can to your confession of conscious faith is the secret to placing subconscious faith in your heart. On the other hand, resisting the urge to confess negative emotions will keep subconscious doubts and fears out of your heart.

When anything good happens in your life, be appreciative of it and give thanks to God for receiving it. You know great things don't happen every day in your life, but you can think every day about the great things that have happened to you in the past. Be grateful for them, remember the joy they brought you, and praise God for them. It goes without saying that you should be doing the same procedure for all the things you believe you are going to receive from the promises of God.

I was raised to believe if you asked God for something and you really wanted it to come about, He might grant your prayer. I now know God grants prayers as a spiritual blessing if we really believe He gave us what we prayed for at the time we prayed; that is, if we can keep from lusting for it.

Don't Lust

It's time to speak of an enemy that can be every bit as dangerous and sneaky as fear and doubt can be when it comes to receiving from the promises of God.

> Let your conversation be without covetousness; and be content with such things as ye have: for he hath said, I will never leave thee, nor forsake thee.
> Hebrews 13:5

When believing God for something, you must be content with the things you have and for the outcome that occurs from believing God. The two hardest things you will face in order to receive from the promises of God are not to doubt and to stay content.

A feeling of discontentment, or a strong desire for something, will compete with the joy that your expectation creates when you think about receiving what you believe God is going to give you. That is being double-minded. Double-minded people should expect nothing from God.

> [6] But let him ask in faith, nothing wavering. For he that wavereth is like a wave of the sea driven with the wind and tossed.
> [7] For let not that man think that he shall receive any thing of the Lord.
> [8] A double minded man is unstable in all his ways.
> James 1:6-8

It's not easy, but you must enjoy and appreciate the thing you believe God is going to give you as if you already have it in the physical world, but you shouldn't be lusting for it.

Strongly wanting something, or lusting, is an invitation for Satan to offer you a physical solution instead of the solution of having faith in God and His written Word. Remember, when you pray and ask God for something, He always gives it to you in the spiritual world at that time as a spiritual blessing. It is the believer's duty to look upon a blessing from God as if it has already manifested in the physical world.

There is a fine line between wanting something and lusting for something. When you believe God for a thing and have confidence, expectation, joy, and peace that you will receive it, then you are doing well. If you become fearful of not receiving it and begin to wonder how or when you are going to be able to receive the thing you believe God is going to do for you, you should be concerned that your desire for it is becoming lust.

Now, as far as how to keep fear and doubt out of your hearts, you must starve the monsters. It is a fact of life that bad things happen, but even so, you should not make bad events in your life bigger than they really are by feeding them with more negative emotions than you absolutely have to. Also, you should not give bad events in your life desserts by dwelling on them long after the fact.

After it is all said and done, it comes down to this. If you want to be prosperous, you need to think like a winner.

For as he thinketh in his heart, so is he: . . .

Proverbs 23:7

Thinking like a winner will cause you to act like a winner. Acting like a winner will cause your own heart to believe that you are a winner. If you think like a winner and act like a winner, you are a winner.

A Deeper Understanding

In this section, readers are presented with a short but well-rounded review of the knowledge needed to successfully operate in the promises of God.

To function as Christians, we all need faith. So how do we obtain faith?

> So then faith cometh by hearing, and hearing by the word of God
>
> Romans 10:17

Our faith comes from Jesus.

> Looking unto Jesus the author and finisher of our faith; who for the joy that was set before him endured the cross, despising the shame, and is set down at the right hand of the throne of God.
>
> Hebrews 12:2

When you hear the Word of God, you have the opportunity to understand the Word of God and to believe in Jesus. If you believe in Jesus and make Him your Lord and Savior, you will receive faith and righteousness from Jesus.

> Even the righteousness of God which is by faith of Jesus Christ unto all and upon all them that believe: for there is no difference:
>
> Romans 3:22

When you have received both faith and righteousness from Jesus, you will find it easier to understand the written Word of

God. Understanding God's written Word makes it possible to believe and to trust God's written promises.

You will need to believe and trust God's written Word in order to have the faith needed to rebuke Satan, which every Christian must do when they stand on the Word of God. Rebuking Satan is necessary to prevent doubting.

> For verily I say unto you, That whosoever shall say unto this mountain, Be thou removed, and be thou cast into the sea; and shall not doubt in his heart, but shall believe that those things which he saith shall come to pass; he shall have whatsoever he saith.
>
> Mark 11:23

> [6] But let him ask in faith, nothing wavering. For he that wavereth is like a wave of the sea driven with the wind and tossed.
> [7] For let not that man think that he shall receive any thing of the Lord.
> [8] A double minded man is unstable in all his ways.
>
> James 1:6-8

Every Christian needs to obey God's written Word and get the sin out of their lives. The more we obey God's written Word, the more power He adds to our faith and our righteousness.

> This book of the law shall not depart out of thy mouth; but thou shalt meditate therein day and night, that thou mayest observe to do according to all that is written therein: for then thou shalt make thy way prosperous, and then thou shalt have good success.
>
> Joshua 1:8

But seek ye first the kingdom of God, and his righteousness; and all these things shall be added unto you.

Matthew 6:33

Confess your faults one to another, and pray one for another, that ye may be healed. The effectual fervent prayer of a righteous man availeth much.

James 5:16

When God has added power to both your faith and to your righteousness, you will find it much easier to trust God's Word concerning prospering His children. Trusting the written Word of God as you stand on God's promises to prosper you creates confidence and expectation.

Having confidence and expectation creates joy and peace in your heart. When you go to the Lord with praises, prayers, and confessions with joy and peace in your heart, God will hear you. To receive from God, you must be heard.

And if we know that he hear us, whatsoever we ask, we know that we have the petitions that we desired of him.

I John 5:15

It should be your goal as a Christian to use the power of Christ to become more and more righteous. The more you become like Jesus in your life, the more righteousness God gives you.

> Thou hypocrite, first cast out the beam out of thine own eye; and then shalt thou see clearly to cast out the mote out of thy brother's eye.
>
> Matthew 7:5

Remember, the prayers of a righteous man avails much (James 5:16).

But before you have the righteousness or the power to help others, you must remove the beam from your own eye, which means you must get the sin out of your life by obeying God's written Word.

Because of Jesus' work on the cross, sin has no authority over believers. If sin wins in our lives, it is because we yield to it. We cannot teach others to use the authority from Jesus to get the sin out of their lives if we have not used it to get the sin out of our own lives.

When you are tempted by sin, confess the following: "In the name of Jesus, sin has no authority over me. I am a child of God."

> Submit yourselves therefore to God. Resist the devil, and he will flee from you.
>
> James 4:7

The Lord wants us to take all of our needs and wants to Him, both big and small.

> Therefore I say unto you, What things soever ye desire, when ye pray, believe that ye receive them, and ye shall have them.
>
> Mark 11:24

After praying and asking the Lord for something, stop wanting whatever you are believing for and replace it with thanksgiving and praise to God. He has already given you what you desired in the form of a spiritual blessing, which will later become a physical blessing. Stop wanting and start receiving.

Unforgiven Sins

While some Christians struggle with forgiving others, many Christians find it extremely difficult to forgive themselves. Most of you know that after God forgives your sins, He no longer remembers them, but you are not God; therefore, it is not easy for you to forgive your own sins, but you must.

> For I will be merciful to their unrighteousness, and their sins and their iniquities will I remember no more.
>
> Hebrew 8:12

As long as you have unforgiven sin in your heart, there will be shame and doubt there also. Your enemy uses your shame and doubt against you to prevent you from receiving what God has already placed in your heart.

> [21] Beloved, if our heart condemn us not, then have we confidence toward God.
> [22] And whatsoever we ask, we receive of him, because we keep his commandments, and do those things that are pleasing in his sight.
> [23] And this is his commandment, That we should believe on the name of his Son Jesus Christ, and love one another, as he gave us commandment.
>
> I John 3:21-23

Having unexpected losses repeatedly happen in your life is a tell-tale sign of unforgiven sin within your heart. Chances are God is not out to punish you, but you are out to punish yourself.

My advice to you is that when your past sins come to your mind, you should say the following out loud if possible. "Yes, in the past I have sinned, but my God has forgiven all of my sins. In Jesus' name I pray, Amen." After a while Satan will get tired of hearing you speak the name of Jesus and will retreat.

> Submit yourselves therefore to God. Resist the devil, and he will flee from you.
>
> James 4:7

Consider this: When Jesus died on the cross to save you from your sins, He gave you victory over your sins, but you still have to pick up your own cross and follow Him. Let me make it clear. You need to use the power and authority of Christ to stop sinning. You must put your sins to death.

> And when he had called the people unto him with his disciples also, he said unto them, Whosoever will come after me, let him deny himself, and take up his cross, and follow me.
>
> Mark 8:34

Jesus did not save you from the fight. He just gave you the ability to win the fight against your sins.

I grew up angry and ashamed. As far as I was concerned, I was damaged goods. School work was next to impossible. Much later in life I discovered dyslexia was my problem but not before I acted out against God and the world.

After I became a Christian, I tried to receive from God's written promises but, sadly, I would fail over and over again. It became obvious to me that unforgiven sin was the problem. I realized that God had forgiven my sins but I hadn't forgiven myself. I needed to place God's forgiveness in my heart by joyfully confessing my thankfulness. Since then, I have had a lot of practice "walking my talk" concerning unforgiven sin in my life. I wouldn't say I have completely fixed my problem, but I have made a rather large dent in it.

Feeling better about yourself is another key to helping you forgive yourself. Become a do-gooder and look for ways to help others. What talents do you have that could be used to help others? Helping others has given me real purpose in my life. It is truly better to give than to receive.

Victory comes to those who refuse to give up. Don't let Satan use past sins to keep you from receiving what God has already given to you in His promises.

From the time I was a little baby until my late twenties, God would intervene in my life to keep me from harm and death. This confused me a great deal because time after time, weird things would happen in my life to keep me from having victories that I believe I earned. Because of all the weird losses I had, I couldn't just blame it on being bad luck, so I blamed them on God, saying over and over again "God hates me."

I now understand God didn't hate me but that I hated myself. It was the negative emotions in my heart that would not let me win. Winning is all about being winners in your heart. I invite you to do as I have done and declare war on all unforgiven sin and every negative feeling in your heart. Cast down all negative thoughts and replace them with positive thoughts.

If you think about it, God knows all of our past sins and all of our future sins. He also knows every one of our faults and weaknesses, but yet He still chooses us to be His very own children. Can't we just love ourselves without feeling guilty?

God forgives our sins by choosing not to remember them anymore. We too must stop thinking about our past sins and learn to forgive ourselves.

Stubborn Unforgiveness

Have you committed sins in the past that were so bad that they made you sick every time you happened to think about them? The sins you cannot believe you would ever do but you did. The sins you beg God to forgive you for but somehow you cannot forgive yourself for. The sins that you are unable to confess to others, even though the Bible tells us we should.

Brothers and sisters in Christ, I have been there and have done that more times than I care to admit. For many years I searched for a solution to this problem, so now please allow me to tell you about what I have found.

First of all, I can tell you for sure that we were set up to fail. We are exactly where Satan wants us to be. We are too ashamed to tell others about our sins even though this would help God to release us from our sins.

Our problem started way back in the Garden of Eden. When Satan spoke to Eve, she received an evil spirit, or a curse. The evil spirit that enticed Eve received power as the result of her imaging that the forbidden fruit was good to eat and that God was wrong about what would happen to them if they ate of it. Once the evil spirit from Satan received power, it caused Eve to believe what she wanted to believe. Eve's evil spirit is now the source of the sin nature of every human who is born.

Sin nature is the ability to believe what we want to believe instead of what is logical. Today we know the evil spirit Eve received from Satan is the man of sin, or the son of perdition.

[1] Now we beseech you, brethren, by the coming of our Lord Jesus Christ, and by our gathering together unto him,

[2] That ye be not soon shaken in mind, or be troubled, neither by spirit, nor by word, nor by letter as from us, as that the day of Christ is at hand.

[3] Let no man deceive you by any means: for that day shall not come, except there come a falling away first, and that man of sin be revealed, the son of perdition;

[4] Who opposeth and exalteth himself above all that is called God, or that is worshipped; so that he as God sitteth in the temple of God, shewing himself that he is God.

[5] Remember ye not, that, when I was yet with you, I told you these things?

[6] And now ye know what withholdeth that he might be revealed in his time.

[7] For the mystery of iniquity doth already work: only he who now letteth will let, until he be taken out of the way.

[8] And then shall that Wicked be revealed, whom the Lord shall consume with the spirit of his mouth, and shall destroy with the brightness of his coming:

[9] Even him, whose coming is after the working of Satan with all power and signs and lying wonders,

[10] And with all deceivableness of unrighteousness in them that perish; because they received not the love of the truth, that they might be saved.

[11] And for this cause God shall send them strong delusion, that they should believe a lie:

¹² That they all might be damned who believed not the truth, but had pleasure in unrighteousness.

II Thessalonians 2:1-12

The man of sin sits in the temple of God where he influences our subconscious minds, which in turn influences our conscious minds.

> And what agreement hath the temple of God with idols? for ye are the temple of the living God; as God hath said, I will dwell in them, and walk in them; and I will be their God, and they shall be my people.
> II Corinthians 6:16

Just like Eve, when anyone of us looks upon forbidden fruit, the man of sin causes the sin of lust to build up in our hearts. Once the fruit is ripe, in a moment of weakness Satan causes us to do what we would never ever do and eat of the fruit.

Satan always comes when we are at our weakest point. Alcohol, drugs, or any negative emotional state creates all the opportunity that Satan needs if we have sin in our hearts.

I don't know your emotional weakness or sin trap, but I do know many of you are just as sorry and ashamed of what you have done as I have been for my past sins.

First, we all must stop digging. Since we are Christians, most of us have stopped digging our sin traps long ago. The inability to confess embarrassing sins to others is a problem. One could consider this problem to be a mountain.

Jesus in His Word told us what we must do about any mountains that we have between us and the ability to receive from God.

> [22] And Jesus answering saith unto them, Have faith in God.
> [23] For verily I say unto you, That whosoever shall say unto this mountain, Be thou removed, and be thou cast into the sea; and shall not doubt in his heart, but shall believe that those things which he saith shall come to pass; he shall have whatsoever he saith.
> [24] Therefore I say unto you, What things soever ye desire, when ye pray, believe that ye receive them, and ye shall have them.
> [25] And when ye stand praying, forgive, if ye have ought against any: that your Father also which is in heaven may forgive you your trespasses.
> [26] But if ye do not forgive, neither will your Father which is in heaven forgive your trespasses.
>
> Mark 11:22-26

Please take note of the verses Mark 11:25-26 where Jesus lets us know that in order for God to forgive our sins, we must forgive others, which includes ourselves.

As mentioned earlier, the man of sin, or the son of perdition, influences our subconscious minds, which in turn influences our conscious minds and is the mountain that we need to speak to. We must cast him into the sea (Mark 11:23). When we speak to the mountain, we need to tell Satan we know he caused us to commit the sin that we have been unable to forgive ourselves for. That act is called naming it, and it is absolutely necessary to do.

Then we need to cast him out in the name of Jesus and tell him he must go into the sea (a spiritual place that was created when God gave the name Seas to gathered waters). For all this to work, we must believe that it does work and it has worked.

My friends, I'm not saying it will be easy, but at least you now know what you need to do to receive the benefits of Mark 11:24 (believing what you prayed for).

In the future, when Satan reminds you of your sins, speak up and remind him of what it says in Mark 11:23 (casting Satan into the sea).

Hidden Unforgiveness

We all know that any unforgiveness we have can create great difficulties in our lives and our walks with God. What many of us don't know however is that we can have unforgiveness that we are not even consciously aware of.

I invite you readers to make a list of five to ten unpleasant events that have happened in your lives. Make a note of the events that create the most negative emotions. Those are the ones you need to give your attention to the most.

Chances are that in the minds of these list makers, there was blame assigned to each one of those unpleasant life events. We are human, and that is what humans do.

For example, let's say when you were about twelve years old, your dog was run over by a truck, and what made matters even worse is that your younger brother had left the gate open. Now fast forward to today. Unconscious unforgiveness could be the root cause of a bad relationship you have with your younger brother. Maybe it is the source of your strange dislike of truck drivers or even trucks themselves.

After examining my own life, I found the need to ask both God and my own mother for forgiveness for blaming both of them for my father's leaving us when I was young. I also recently forgave referees from two different sports events that happened when I was playing football and running track in high school. Don't laugh. Those two events really hurt me. Memories of victories turning into defeats can leave deep scars.

There is little doubt that some of the readers of this book will have their lives changed for the better once they have revealed and forgiven their hidden unforgivenesses.

Beware of Missing Links

This week your preacher may preach a sermon on faith or righteousness. Whatever the subject is, it could be the best sermon on that subject you have ever heard.

When it comes to receiving prosperity from the written promises of God, chances are you will fail to receive it if you don't rely on all of your preacher's sermons on prosperity.

Picture yourself being down a deep well of need and lack. Lucky for you there is a rope reaching all the way to the top where there is plenty.

The rope is created from smaller ropes that are linked together. The small pieces of rope are all the good sermons on prosperity you have heard over the years. Know for certain if there is a link or two missing in the rope; that is, if there are messages you have not heard or have not put to work in your life, you will not reach the top of the rope to the land of plenty. You will not receive from your faith in God's written promises.

I have met many good Christians who don't believe in prosperity from God's promises. When I ask them why, they usually say they have tried to receive from God's promises but it did not work for them.

I understand where they are coming from. Until I found my missing links and put them to work in my life, I too would fail over and over again.

Brothers and sisters in Christ, there are no missing links in *God's Prosperity Promises*, but you need to put all of the lessons into effect in your life.

Please remember, God wants to give His children better lives, but the main purpose of God's promises is for the prospering of our souls.

> Beloved, I wish above all things that thou mayest
> prosper and be in health, even as thy soul prospereth.
> III John 1:2

If we were to be honest with ourselves, we usually know what our missing links are and what we must do to defeat them, but it doesn't hurt to ask your spouse or friends about your faults and weaknesses. My loved ones are always ready to give me an earful, most of the time without me even having to ask them to.

We need to do the things we know God wants us to do so we can receive the promises of God. Doing this will make us better people. What Christian doesn't want to become a better person?

Spiritual Blessings

> The blessing of the LORD, it maketh rich, and he addeth no sorrow with it.
>
> > Proverbs 10:22

Spiritual blessings are the sources of physical blessings.

When you pray to God and ask Him for something that is according to His will or according to His written Word, He will give it to you in the form of a spiritual blessing.

> For all the promises of God in him are yea, and in him Amen, unto the glory of God by us.
>
> > II Corinthians 1:20

> If ye abide in me, and my words abide in you, ye shall ask what ye will, and it shall be done unto you.
>
> > John 15:7

A spiritual blessing from God has two parts. The first part of the blessing gives the receiver of the blessing the ability to do what they must do in order to be eligible to receive the second part of the blessing.

The second part of a blessing gives the receiver the ability to speak words with the power to rule or influence people or events, which they normally have no power over. You only receive the second part of a blessing if God judges your works, deeds, and faith level high enough to receive what you prayed for.

In the parable of "The Talents" in Matthew 25:14-30 and Luke 19:11-27, you can see that with the first part of a spiritual blessing you only have power and authority to work in your own field or life. The power and authority to rule over many things within the second part of a spiritual blessing is not given to you unless God judges your work and faith level to be high enough.

14 For the kingdom of heaven is as a man travelling into a far country, who called his own servants, and delivered unto them his goods.

15 And unto one he gave five talents, to another two, and to another one; to every man according to his several ability; and straightway took his journey.

16 Then he that had received the five talents went and traded with the same, and made them other five talents.

17 And likewise he that had received two, he also gained other two.

18 But he that had received one went and digged in the earth, and hid his lord's money.

19 After a long time the lord of those servants cometh, and reckoneth with them.

20 And so he that had received five talents came and brought other five talents, saying, Lord, thou deliveredst unto me five talents: behold, I have gained beside them five talents more.

21 His lord said unto him, Well done, thou good and faithful servant: thou hast been faithful over a few things, I will make thee ruler over many things: enter thou into the joy of thy lord.

22 He also that had received two talents came and said, Lord, thou deliveredst unto me two talents: behold, I have gained two other talents beside them.

²³ His lord said unto him, Well done, good and faithful servant; thou hast been faithful over a few things, I will make thee ruler over many things: enter thou into the joy of thy lord.

²⁴ Then he which had received the one talent came and said, Lord, I knew thee that thou art an hard man, reaping where thou hast not sown, and gathering where thou hast not strawed:

²⁵ And I was afraid, and went and hid thy talent in the earth: lo, there thou hast that is thine.

²⁶ His lord answered and said unto him, Thou wicked and slothful servant, thou knewest that I reap where I sowed not, and gather where I have not strawed:

²⁷ Thou oughtest therefore to have put my money to the exchangers, and then at my coming I should have received mine own with usury.

²⁸ Take therefore the talent from him, and give it unto him which hath ten talents.

²⁹ For unto every one that hath shall be given, and he shall have abundance: but from him that hath not shall be taken away even that which he hath.

³⁰ And cast ye the unprofitable servant into outer darkness: there shall be weeping and gnashing of teeth.

Matthew 25:14-30

When you pray and ask God for things, you cannot expect to receive what you prayed for until you have exercised your faith by preparing your own fields and seeding them.

In simple terms, you must use the blessings of God to rule over the things you think, say, and do in your own fields or life before you can use the second part of a spiritual blessing to influence or to rule over the things you normally have no rule over.

You must remove the beam from your own eyes before you can see clearly to remove the mote from others' eyes (Matthew 7:3-5).

This example may be helpful to you. I want to help many others have better lives. I want to do this by living my life in accordance to God's written Word and then by selling many helpful books; therefore, I need to use the ability that God gave me and the blessings He gave me to overcome the sins in my life and to write a book that is good enough to be judged worthy by God.

If or when my works are judged worthy by God, He will give the words that I speak the power and authority to influence people to want to purchase my book.

How to Win

As previously stated, when you pray and ask God for anything that is according to His will, which is His written Word, He always gives you what you pray for in the form of spiritual blessings within your heart. Everything you pray for has a certain level of faith strength required to receive it.

If your faith's strength level is not high enough to receive what you prayed for, Satan will come and test you to give your strength level an opportunity to increase. When faith tests are passed, your faith strength levels will increase in your heart and you will have more power with God.

Wise Christians don't confess their faith test losses. They confess the Word of God as truth and that they have received what they prayed for. They do so because God has already given them what they prayed for in the form of spiritual blessings within their hearts.

Every time faith in the written Word of God is confessed instead of the truth of this world, believers' faith strength levels increase. After a while, their faith strength levels will reach the required level and they will receive in the physical world what they already received in their hearts as spiritual blessings.

When God gives a spiritual blessing, He sees it as real, or a done deal, which makes sense because God is Spirit and He is real.

We are physical beings; therefore, we see blessings as real if they are physical. For a spiritual blessing to become a physical blessing, we must see it as God sees it. We must see spiritual blessings as real, or physical. In order for us to see spiritual blessings as physical things, our faith strength level has to be at the required level.

Concerning receiving from God's prosperity promises in His written Word, due season only occurs when our faith power level reaches the required strength. Christians need to know how to increase their faith strength levels so they can arrive at due season.

Hearing God's written Word gives you the opportunity to understand and to believe God's promises. The understanding and believing of God's written Word is your faith. The confessing of your faith and the obedience to God's written Word will cause faith to form in your heart. Faith in your heart is a great thing, but to have power it must be tested by Satan and be judged by God. To pass a faith test, you must trust, obey, and confess God's written Word instead of what you see or feel in the physical world.

If you pass a faith test, your faith strength level will increase, but if you fail a faith test, it will cause your faith strength level to decrease. Getting upset after a faith test failure (trial, temptation, or loss) and confessing that you have lost will cause you to lose faith. On the other hand, trusting, obeying, and confessing God's written Word as truth after having a loss will cause your faith strength level to increase. Even the higher faith strength levels can be reached by doing right things after having losses. Old Testament Job is a perfect example of this principle. He lost everything that he owned but still came out as a winner.

> [10] And the LORD turned the captivity of Job, when he prayed for his friends: also the LORD gave Job twice as much as he had before.

¹¹ Then came there unto him all his brethren, and all his sisters, and all they that had been of his acquaintance before, and did eat bread with him in his house: and they bemoaned him, and comforted him over all the evil that the LORD had brought upon him: every man also gave him a piece of money, and every one an earring of gold.

¹² So the LORD blessed the latter end of Job more than his beginning: for he had fourteen thousand sheep, and six thousand camels, and a thousand yoke of oxen, and a thousand she asses.

¹³ He had also seven sons and three daughters.

¹⁴ And he called the name of the first, Jemima; and the name of the second, Kezia; and the name of the third, Kerenhappuch.

¹⁵ And in all the land were no women found so fair as the daughters of Job: and their father gave them inheritance among their brethren.

¹⁶ After this lived Job an hundred and forty years, and saw his sons, and his sons' sons, even four generations.

¹⁷ So Job died, being old and full of days.

Job 42:10-17

Like Job, we cannot prevent defeats and losses in our lives, but we can get double for our trouble by doing the righteous things when they occur.

Don't Sabotage Your Victories

God required the Jewish Nation to celebrate victories when they had them and to keep remembering them at later times. He wanted their victories to get down into their hearts so they could draw strength from them, which would help give them more victories in the future.

In order for us to have more victories in the future, we must also get our victories down into our hearts by celebrating them after we receive them and then continuing to remember them often after that.

My mother was a creative and industrial-type person. Time and time again she would get financial victories in her life and then turn around and make decisions that would sabotage her victories. I remember at least one time asking her why she made the decisions she did, and she told me she felt she had to but didn't know exactly why.

Because of what I read in the Bible about the Jewish Nation, I believe she could not hold onto her victories because she didn't let them get down into her heart before moving on to more challenges.

Don't move on after your victories until you get them down into your heart by celebrating them, because you are going to need past victories to draw upon in order to give you future victories.

In the past I made the same mistakes as my mother. After having victories in my life, I too moved on to other challenges before getting my wins down into my heart.

Later, when life presented me with larger challenges to my goals, I would fail just like my mother. Today, I take the time to celebrate all new victories and to remember my past wins.

How to Test Your Faith

Do you want to know if your faith is strong enough to receive what you are believing God's written promises for? Answering a few questions honestly can tell you all you need to know about your faith.

Do you really expect to receive from God what you asked Him for, or are you just hoping for it? Be honest with yourself. Having expectation is the direct consequence of believing without doubting. If you don't have expectation, there is a problem with your faith.

There are two main reasons for weak faith. The first reason is a lack of trust in God's written Word. The second reason is a condemning heart.

The lack of trust in the Bible usually comes from the lack of truly understanding what is written in God's Word, or it could come from the lack of believing and trusting in what Jesus was able to accomplish on the cross.

Spending time and effort in studying and meditating on the Word of God will create faith in both the Bible and Jesus' work on the cross. Real trust only comes after meaningful understanding.

Chances are good that a condemning heart is the reason for weak faith. There are many reasons for a condemning heart; such as not living your life according to the Bible, evil thoughts and deeds, or not giving tithes and offerings to God. The most likely reason of all is you have unforgiven sin in your life. This is past sin which God has forgiven you for but you cannot seem to forgive yourself for.

When you ask God to forgive your sins, He does it at that time and never remembers them again. You too should resist the temptation of remembering the past sins God has already forgiven you for. If you don't choose to stop remembering your past sins, a condemning heart will always be a part of your future.

Doing God's will and helping others in need will help heal a condemning heart, but until you are able to stop thinking about your past sins, you will always struggle with a condemning heart.

Having expectation can tell you if your faith is strong enough to receive from the promises of God, but how can you know if your expectation is strong enough to receive?

In a word, the answer is "joy." If your expectation is at a healthy level, it will produce joy. Having joy is evidence of expectation and that you believe you will receive the promise.

It is written that faith is the evidence of things not seen (Hebrews 11:1). I suggest if your faith does not produce expectation and your expectation does not produce joy, maybe your faith really is just hopeful thinking.

Don't get me wrong though. Hopeful thinking can be a good thing to have, especially if a person is living their life according to what is written in the Bible and is sowing good seed.

We reap what we sow (Galatians 6:7). Sowing good seed in life will eventually create good harvest. Good harvests or victories down in your heart can be used to increase your faith, expectation, and joy.

I know of two ways to create the joy of expectation. The first way is to remember the joy of previous victories. The second way is to imagine victories and confess in the name of Jesus that God has already given you the victory.

Your subconscious mind cannot tell the difference between an imagined event and a real event, so the joy you create with your imagination is real. Don't let the lack of previous victories keep you from having joy. God has given you an imagination, so use it.

When it comes to receiving from God's written prosperity promises, you know you are on the right track if you have faith, expectation, and joy.

Daydream Your Way to Joy in Your Heart

Have you ever noticed that joyful people seem to have good things happening in their lives all the time? Do you think they are happy because of the good things happening to them, or could it be that because they are always happy, good things keep happening to them?

Of course the answer is that both things are happening at the same time, but there is more to it than that because in life, both good things and bad things happen to everyone.

Your future is determined by the way you handle events in your life, by your attitudes toward those events, and by the words you speak. You really do reap what you sow.

Joy in your heart will help cause joy to develop in your life and is an essential element for receiving from God's prosperity promises. Positive daydreaming is all about putting joy in your heart.

Having positive daydreams about the things you are believing God for takes practice to do correctly. Only joyful thoughts can be allowed to stay around. All negative thoughts must be cast down and replaced with joyful thoughts.

Avoid questions of any kind, such as those that involve "what if?" and "what about?" They can lead to doubts and fears.

Positive daydreaming is a great way to create joy and success in your life. The next time you find yourself not doing anything, do something useful. You should daydream like a child, a child of God.

Finally, brethren, whatsoever things are true, whatsoever things are honest, whatsoever things are just, whatsoever things are pure, whatsoever things are lovely, whatsoever things are of good report; if there be any virtue, and if there be any praise, think on these things.

Philippians 4:8

Defeating Double-Mindedness

We are returning to the subject of double-mindedness because it is just that important. Those who suffer from double-mindedness will not receive anything from God.

> ⁶ But let him ask in faith, nothing wavering. For he that wavereth is like a wave of the sea driven with the wind and tossed.
> ⁷ For let not that man think that he shall receive any thing of the Lord.
> ⁸ A double minded man is unstable in all his ways.
>
> James 1:6-8

Every one of us has wrestled with an important decision, decided on a course of action, acted on our decision, and then wondered if we made the right choice. That, my friend, is double-mindedness.

The fact is that any action taken when we have double-mindedness is a sin. It doesn't matter if we choose the right answer or not. If we have fear or double-mindedness, we lack faith, and that is a sin.

> And he that doubteth is damned if he eat, because he eateth not of faith: for whatsoever is not of faith is sin.
>
> Romans 14:23

Having fear is not a sin, but acting upon that fear is a sin. Cast down fear in the name of Jesus before acting upon any decision you have to make, and be ready to do it again if Satan returns.

We Christians know that when making an important decision, the wise thing to do is to pray to God and ask Him to lead us to the right answer. What many of us fail to realize is that God gives us what we pray for as a spiritual blessing at the very time we pray. If we can keep our faith in God and keep the peace of God, we will receive what we pray for here in the physical world.

Between the time we receive God's spiritual blessing and the time we receive the blessing in the physical, Satan will come to test our faith. He knows if he can get us to doubt or have fear, we will lose our peace about the thing we are believing God for.

Beware of seemingly harmless little questions like: "Did God really say that?", "Did I make the right decision?" or "Will I ever get what I prayed for?" Questions and second guessing our choices are peace killers. They must be avoided at all cost. If possible, don't make any decision unless you can keep from doubting about your choice. Guard your peace in your decisions. Satan will come to test you, so be ready.

Has the following ever happened to you? You prayed to God for help in making a decision, you received an answer you believed God had given you because of the peace you felt, and then after a while you started to doubt that you really had heard from God. Because of this, you ended up deciding against the decision you once believed God had given to you and then, to your surprise, you ended up feeling peace about your second decision. Chances are the second peace you felt was a false peace. It didn't come from God, but Satan was its author.

Giving into fear and doubt can be a relief that can seem like peace. Can you imagine the relief Moses would have felt if he didn't have to face the Pharaoh? Surely it would have felt like peace to him, but of course giving into fear would have led to failure.

When you pray to God for direction, He is going to give you the right answer. Many times the right answer from God will take you out of your comfort zone. Don't be fooled into thinking the relief you felt when you decided to stay in your comfort zone was peace from God.

If you are going back and forth on a decision, ask yourself which peace is real, which one is false, which one is based on faith in God, and which one is based on fear and doubt about yourself. You will be glad you did.

Know this: improving your decision-making ability can take you a long way down the road to success.

Escaping from Temptation

I know what it feels like to desperately want to stop sinning in an area of my life only to give into that temptation over and over again. I also know what I did to escape my sin trap. The same method could work for you, and it is not even complicated.

In very simple terms you must speak faith-filled words from your heart at the time of a temptation. The challenge is how to get faith-filled words into your heart in order to speak them out. Fortunately for us, the Bible clearly states what must be done.

> My heart is inditing a good matter: I speak of the things which I have made touching the king: my tongue is the pen of a ready writer.
>
> Psalm 45:1

Speaking faith-filled words with confidence, joy, and peace will place these words into your heart. I routinely confess the following words throughout the day to prepare me for the time that I am faced with "this mountain" or temptation. "By the power within the name of Jesus I will not (name your temptation), I will not (name your temptation), I will not (name your temptation). Thank you, Lord Jesus, for saving me from my sins."

If you prefer, please feel free to create your own confession, but just be sure to confess it often throughout the day.

In the past after I repeatedly confessed my faith and then had temptation, I thought it meant I had lost my faith battle, but I was wrong. The coming of a temptation is when the battle begins. That is when we speak the faith-filled words we placed in our hearts. Each victory and loss is a battle. Sometimes many battles must be won before the war can be won.

If you lose a battle, all is not lost. Ask God to forgive you and then forgive yourself and keep on making your confessions daily. Confessing your faith-filled words after a loss, instead of what Satan wants you to say, will cause your faith to grow. If you don't give up, you will win. God guarantees you will win the war, but He doesn't guarantee you will win every battle.

If the preceding method of escaping sin fails to work for you, you are in serious trouble. Fortunately, Jesus has some good advice for any of us who find ourselves entrapped by sin.

> [8] Wherefore if thy hand or thy foot offend thee, cut them off, and cast them from thee: it is better for thee to enter into life halt or maimed, rather than having two hands or two feet to be cast into everlasting fire.
> [9] And if thine eye offend thee, pluck it out, and cast it from thee: it is better for thee to enter into life with one eye, rather than having two eyes to be cast into hell fire.
>
> Matthew 18:8-9

Allow me to tell you what I believe the preceding Bible verses mean. I believe that cutting off a hand or foot means to stop doing the activity where you can't control yourself while doing it. An example of this would be that if you have an alcoholic problem where you can't stop drinking, you need to stop drinking alcohol altogether. Don't even think about taking that first drink. Don't even go to any place that alcohol is being served, such as a bar or party.

Then I believe plucking out your eye means that you shouldn't look upon the thing that tempts you. An example of this would be that if pornography is your downfall, don't go near anything that would tempt you to do wrong, such as looking at porn magazines, watching certain TV shows, looking at pornography on the internet, or even going to the beach. In drastic cases you may even have to abstain from having sexual relations altogether if your spouse consents to doing that in order to help you.

Jesus didn't say it would be easy, but that it would be worth it. Practicing the previously mentioned method for escaping temptation will make following Jesus' harsh advice of cutting off our hand or foot or plucking out our eye easier for us when we are dealing with the problem.

Faith Walls

Are you presently facing a faith wall? All those who walk in faith will eventually come to one.

Faith walls are the times in our lives when it is impossible for us to see a path to a victory or a good outcome. They are never fun. I don't know of any Christian in my life that hasn't faced at least one faith wall. Many of us would love if we only had one to face.

I'm sure that every one of us has prayed to God for something and then after believing but seeing no results came to a place where we couldn't see how a victory could ever be possible without a miracle happening. Am I right? I remember in the past that when I came to a faith wall, I thought it was God's way of saying "no," but I was wrong.

God provides faith walls in our lives to give our faith the opportunity to receive the power of God so that we can influence others and the circumstances which we normally have no power over.

Facing down faith walls is the method where God has chosen a way to give us His power to receive glory for Him and righteousness for us. Every Christian needs righteousness to have clothing in heaven.

Someday we will be invited to a great wedding feast in heaven. At that time, we will need wedding garments. The righteousness we receive by causing the Lord to receive glory is our new heavenly body.

Confessing the Word of God with confidence, expectation, joy, and peace will place God's written Word within our hearts. At some time, God will judge what we placed in our hearts and give us power to influence others and change circumstances like only God can do.

Waiting is hard, but waiting when the path to victory cannot be seen is especially hard and even impossible without having faith in God and His written Word.

I pray that this book has helped provide you with the understanding you need to keep your faith during your faith tests. Now use the faith ladder I have provided and climb over your faith walls. Victory awaits you on the other side.

Imaginary Conversations with the Lord

The following section was written to help facilitate understandings of how to receive prosperity from God. It was designed to be both informative and light-hearted.

<u>Bob – a Christian Man</u>

Lord, after becoming saved five years ago, I have come to you many times in prayer asking You to meet my needs and desires as Your written Word says I should. I have been giving tithes and offerings, and I am trying my best to live according to your written Word; but even after doing all these things, my needs are not being met. Lord, I don't know what to do. Why aren't You meeting my needs?

Actually, Bob, I have answered your prayers and have given you what you asked Me for.

I haven't seen your blessings, Lord. Why can't I see them?

Of course you haven't seen them. I am Spirit; therefore, the blessings I gave to you are spiritual blessings. It is your job to receive them into the physical world.

I am confused, Lord. What must I do?

That was the right question to ask, Bob. You are doing a lot of things right in My sight, but there are some things you need to stop doing. Also, there are some things you need to start doing in your life.

What are the things I'm doing right, Lord?

You believe in My completed work on Calvary, and you have accepted My written Word as the absolute truth. Also, you live your life to the best of your ability in line with the Bible, My written Word.

So, Lord, what are the things I need to stop doing?

You need to control your negative thoughts by not thinking and confessing them. You are worrying a lot about how you are going to pay your bills, especially the unexpected bills that you receive. Worrying, doubting, and fearing is having faith in a bad future and lacking trust in Me and My written Word. It is also a big source of your financial problems, including the unexpected bills.

That hurts to hear, but at least I now know what I have been doing wrong. Thank you, Lord.

You can't stop having thoughts, but you can choose to cast down the negative thoughts and replace them with positive thoughts. Your life will become much better after a time if you will accomplish this deed.

Yes, Lord, I know I need to be a more positive person and with Your help I will try doing better.

You have not lost all the spiritual blessings I have given you over the years though. They are just waiting for a way to become physical in nature. For that to happen, they need a place to come to in physical form.

What do you mean by a place to come to? Can't they just come to me?

100

Bob, you need a field to receive your blessings. Also, since they are spiritual, they cannot just come to you in the physical world. Picture a farmer who gives tithes and offerings to his local church and then plants seed in his fields. It is My pleasure to bless his spiritual seed to cause his physical seed to grow and prosper. If the farmer did not prepare a physical field and plant physical seed, he would not receive My spiritual blessings, nor would he receive a harvest in the fall. Just like the farmer, you will not receive a harvest, Bob, unless you prepare a field and plant seed.

Where is my physical field, Lord, and what kind of seed should I plant?

That is something you will have to find out for yourself, but if you pray I will help you. Your lack of planting a field is the main reason you have many years of spiritual blessings waiting for you.

Please help me find my field, Lord. I work at a place with no hope of job advancement.

Search your heart, Bob. Is there anything you think you might like doing for a living with the possibility of producing a better harvest in the future? Learning a trade or pursuing education should never be overlooked. Sometimes hobbies and investments can become productive fields. Remember, Bob, when you find your field, you need to plant both spiritual seed and physical seed. Be sure to water your seed with confessions of your faith.

What can I do? I don't have enough money for seed.

Physical seed and spiritual seed usually don't have to be money. Education, training, volunteer work, good deeds, and many other things can often make really good seed. Just be creative.

What else should I be doing?

Bob, you need to confess from a faith-filled heart what I have given to you before you get it in physical form. You need to do this without having any doubts about whether you will receive it or not.

How can I place faith in my heart?

Bob, confessing joyfully what I have given to you will place faith in your heart. Joy and peace come from confidence in the truthfulness of My written Word and from the expectation that you will receive from My written promises. Confidence in My written Word comes from understanding, believing, and trusting My written Word. Now if you are having trouble understanding, believing, and trusting My written Word, you need to remove the beam from your eye, which is another way of saying to get the sin out of your life.

Is there anything else I need to know and do to have stronger faith?

Yes, Bob, there is something else. In this life you will have trials, tribulations, and losses. You are good at thinking about past wins in your life and giving Me credit, but when it comes to losses, you are missing great opportunities to build your faith, because you are pouting over those losses.

Confessing the truthfulness and power of My written Word at times of trial, tribulations, and losses is a magnificent way to make your faith stronger. My written Word is full of stories about My faithful servants who received great victories because they did the righteous things after suffering great tribulations.

Every Christian knows the story of Job. He never doubted Me even after suffering great losses. Job's faith was tested by Satan and judged by Me. His faith became twice as strong, and he received double for his trouble.

Lord, did you allow Satan to test Job to give him an opportunity to have more power in heaven?

Yes, Bob, Job already had everything he needed or could use on earth.

I knew there had to be a good reason for You allowing Job to be tempted by Satan like that.

Bob, I know you have been wondering why after you prayed and gave offerings that unexpected bills would come your way.

Yes, Lord, I have wondered about that.

I permitted Satan to test you because you needed stronger faith to receive the things you were asking Me for.

Bob, there is another thing we need to talk about. You asked Me to forgive all your sins and I did, but you haven't forgiven yourself. You have complete faith in the truthfulness of My written Word and My power and willingness to do all

that I promise to do in My Word, but you lack confidence that you will personally receive from My written promises.

You have past sins that you are so ashamed of that, even though you have confessed them to Me, you will not or cannot confess to others. The spiritual blessings I gave to you are always yours even if you don't receive them until you reach heaven. The truth is, Bob, you yourself will prevent blessings from reaching you in the physical world until you can forgive yourself. Confessing your sins to others whom you trust is a way to help you to forgive yourself. I already forgave you, son.

Lord, I am too ashamed of my past sins to tell anyone about them. What should I do?

Confessing your sins to others is the wise thing to do, Bob, but if you cannot do so, do the following: Pray and ask Me for the ability to forgive your unforgiven sins. Then say out loud "God has forgiven me, and in the name of Jesus, I forgive myself." Satan will not give up without a fight. Be prepared to make this confession often.

Lord, why do I have such a hard time forgiving myself?

The answer is simple. It's because you keep remembering your sins. If I did not choose to forget your sins, I would find it very difficult to forgive you too. Bob, cast your thoughts about your past sins down and replace them with the fact that I have already forgiven you and that I don't remember them anymore. Satan has been lying to you. He told you that you must think about past sins to prevent you from sinning again. The truth is that the more you think about your past sins, the more likely you will do them again.

Thank you, Lord, that really helps, but would you tell me why I can't seem to make right decisions? Even after praying and asking You to lead me to right answers and after receiving what I believed was your peace, I still make the wrong decisions. Why can't I receive right answers from you, Lord?

Bob, I did give you right answers.

Then why did I get bad results when I acted upon what I thought were the answers you gave me?

Because Satan stole your peace, Bob. After I gave you the correct answers, you second-guessed them. One cannot keep My peace and second-guess My answers. That is double-mindedness. No one can receive from Me if they are double-minded.

Lord, I always believed if I chose the right answer or best way to proceed that success would follow.

Bob, the truth is nonbelievers who don't second-guess their choices have a better chance of being successful than believers who are double-minded.

You have given me so much to think about. There are so many other people at my church who could benefit from all that You have given me. Will You show Pastor Jack what you have shared with me?

Write a letter to your pastor and tell him everything we have been talking about, and tell him I will be coming to him.

Okay, Lord, I will.

Pastor Jack

Wake up, Jack. I wish to speak to you

Is that really you, Lord?

Yes, Jack, what do you think of Bob's letter?

I compared it to Your written Word, and it is all in agreement with it.

Yes, that is good, but what did you think of it?

Well, Lord, the understanding in Bob's letter will help many people, but it bothers me that I didn't have the complete picture until now. It especially bothers me that I didn't understand that everyone needs fields to plant both spiritual seed and physical seed in. Why didn't I see this before?

Jack, you can only give to others what I have given to you. I chose to wait until now to share this message with you. You know, Jack, that since you have received this understanding of My written Word, you are now responsible to give this message to your flock.

Yes, Lord, I will gladly do it; but, Lord, many of my fellow preachers don't believe in preaching your prosperity promises. Are they wrong?

They believe in their hearts it is wrong to preach prosperity; therefore, it would be wrong for them to do so. Many preachers believe I am only concerned with prospering their souls. Jack, do you know why there are so many prosperity promises in my written Word?

It's because you love Your children, and You desire them to have better lives.

Yes, Jack, you are right that I do love My children and want them to have good lives on earth, but there is much more to it than that alone. Above all else, I desire for My children's souls to prosper. Learning and doing everything they need to do to receive from My written promises is a wonderful way to prosper souls.

How so, Lord?

For everything My children pray for, there is a certain level of faith they need in order to receive it. For large and more difficult items, their faith level will also need to be large or more powerful. Jack, know this, if their faith level is not high enough to receive what they believe I am going to do for them, Satan will come to give them an opportunity to increase their faith level.

I never thought about Satan's tests in that way, Lord. Believing You for things really could cause the soul to prosper.

Jack, there is one other thing I want to talk to you about, which is the term "due season." Due season has less to do with time than the level of one's faith concerning when one receives from My written promises. Due season comes only when one's faith level reaches the required level.

Waiting on due season is hard work, Lord.

Yes, Jack, I know. Mankind's stumbling block has always been waiting. That's because they have always been

concerned with when and how they would receive from Me. In doing so, they opened the door for the Deceiver.

I know what You are saying is true, Lord, but like I said before, waiting is really hard.

When and how they receive from My written promises belongs to Me. I am God. Mankind needs to be concerned with increasing their faith level to what is needed for them to receive.

What should believers do, Lord?

Believers need to do what they know they should do. Don't wait for Me to tell them what they should do when they know they should do it, and they should always be ready to confess and obey My written Word when Satan comes to test them, which he will do.

What is the most important thing believers need to do when waiting for due season, Lord?

Believers need to believe and confess that they have received what they prayed for, which is the truth since I have given it to them as a spiritual blessing at the time they prayed. Believers put too much importance on receiving it in the physical world and not enough on receiving it in the spiritual world as a spiritual blessing. If they would do this one thing better, due season would come much sooner for them.

Yes, Lord, I see what You are saying now. Thank you for all that you have revealed to me. I will be sure to share it with many others.

That's wonderful, Jack. Good night.

Good night, Lord.

Powerful Prosperity Promises

Old Testament

While the earth remaineth, seedtime and harvest, and cold and heat, and summer and winter, and day and night shall not cease.

Genesis 8:22

But thou shalt remember the LORD thy God: for it is he that giveth thee power to get wealth, that he may establish his covenant which he sware unto thy fathers, as it is this day.

Deuteronomy 8:18

The LORD shall command the blessing upon thee in thy storehouses, and in all that thou settest thine hand unto; and he shall bless thee in the land which the LORD thy God giveth thee.

Deuteronomy 28:8

And the LORD shall make thee plenteous in goods, in the fruit of thy body, and in the fruit of thy cattle, and in the fruit of thy ground, in the land which the LORD sware unto thy fathers to give thee.

Deuteronomy 28:11

This book of the law shall not depart out of thy mouth; but thou shalt meditate therein day and night, that thou mayest observe to do according to all that is written therein: for then thou shalt make thy way prosperous, and then thou shalt have good success.

Joshua 1:8

[1] Blessed is the man that walketh not in the counsel of the ungodly, nor standeth in the way of sinners, nor sitteth in the seat of the scornful.

[2] But his delight is in the law of the LORD; and in his law doth he meditate day and night.

[3] And he shall be like a tree planted by the rivers of water, that bringeth forth his fruit in his season; his leaf also shall not wither; and whatsoever he doeth shall prosper.

Psalms 1:1-3

The young lions do lack, and suffer hunger: but they that seek the LORD shall not want any good thing.

Psalms 34:10

Let them shout for joy, and be glad, that favour my righteous cause: yea, let them say continually, Let the LORD be magnified, which hath pleasure in the prosperity of his servant.

Psalms 35:27

[4] Delight thyself also in the LORD: and he shall give thee the desires of thine heart.

[5] Commit thy way unto the LORD; trust also in him; and he shall bring it to pass.

Psalms 37:4-5

[20] I lead in the way of righteousness, in the midst of the paths of judgment:

[21] That I may cause those that love me to inherit substance; and I will fill their treasures.

Proverbs 8:20-21

The blessing of the LORD, it maketh rich, and he addeth no sorrow with it.

Proverbs 10:22

[20] A man's belly shall be satisfied with the fruit of his mouth; and with the increase of his lips shall he be filled.

[21] Death and life are in the power of the tongue: and they that love it shall eat the fruit thereof.

Proverbs 18:20-21

Bring ye all the tithes into the storehouse, that there may be meat in mine house, and prove me now herewith, saith the LORD of hosts, if I will not open you the windows of heaven, and pour you out a blessing, that there shall not be room enough to receive it.

Malachi 3:10

New Testament

[3] But when thou doest alms, let not thy left hand know what thy right hand doeth:

[4] That thine alms may be in secret: and thy Father which seeth in secret himself shall reward thee openly.

Matthew 6:3-4

113

[19] Lay not up for yourselves treasures upon earth, where moth and rust doth corrupt, and where thieves break through and steal:

[20] But lay up for yourselves treasures in heaven, where neither moth nor rust doth corrupt, and where thieves do not break through nor steal:

[21] For where your treasure is, there will your heart be also.

Matthew 6:19-21

Wherefore, if God so clothe the grass of the field, which to day is, and to morrow is cast into the oven, shall he not much more clothe you, O ye of little faith?

Matthew 6:30

But seek ye first the kingdom of God, and his righteousness; and all these things shall be added unto you.

Matthew 6:33

Jesus said unto him, If thou canst believe, all things are possible to him that believeth.

Mark 9:23

[23] For verily I say unto you, That whosoever shall say unto this mountain, Be thou removed, and be thou cast into the sea; and shall not doubt in his heart, but shall believe that those things which he saith shall come to pass; he shall have whatsoever he saith.

[24] Therefore I say unto you, What things soever ye desire, when ye pray, believe that ye receive them, and ye shall have them.

Mark 11:23-24

Give, and it shall be given unto you; good measure, pressed down, and shaken together, and running over, shall men give into your bosom. For with the same measure that ye mete withal it shall be measured to you again.

Luke 6:38

If ye abide in me, and my words abide in you, ye shall ask what ye will, and it shall be done unto you.

John 15:7

And in that day ye shall ask me nothing. Verily, verily, I say unto you, Whatsoever ye shall ask the Father in my name, he will give it you.

John 16:23

For all the promises of God in him are yea, and in him Amen, unto the glory of God by us.

II Corinthians 1:20

[6] But this I say, He which soweth sparingly shall reap also sparingly; and he which soweth bountifully shall reap also bountifully.

115

[7] Every man according as he purposeth in his heart, so let him give; not grudgingly, or of necessity: for God loveth a cheerful giver.

II Corinthians 9:6-7

Be not deceived; God is not mocked: for whatsoever a man soweth, that shall he also reap.

Galatians 6:7

And let us not be weary in well doing: for in due season we shall reap, if we faint not.

Galatians 6:9

But my God shall supply all your need according to his riches in glory by Christ Jesus.

Philippians 4:19

[35] Cast not away therefore your confidence, which hath great recompence of reward.
[36] For ye have need of patience, that, after ye have done the will of God, ye might receive the promise.

Hebrews 10:35-36

[21] Beloved, if our heart condemn us not, then have we confidence toward God.
[22] And whatsoever we ask, we receive of him, because we keep his commandments, and do those things that are pleasing in his sight.

I John 3:21-22

[14] And this is the confidence that we have in him, that, if we ask any thing according to his will, he heareth us:

[15] And if we know that he hear us, whatsoever we ask, we know that we have the petitions that we desired of him.

I John 5:14-15

Beloved, I wish above all things that thou mayest prosper and be in health, even as thy soul prospereth.

III John 2

Be a Light

Be a light to your family, friends, church, and the world. Lead them out of the darkness of lack, need, and weak faith. You know the way. You have received all the understanding you need.

Let your loved ones motivate you. Think about the joy of helping others to help themselves. Teach them how to fish, or in this case, show them how to receive from the promises of God. Be a hero, tell your friends and loved ones about *God's Prosperity Promises,* or better yet give them a copy of this life-changing book. What person in your life could really use a copy of this book?

God is real and so are His written promises to us, His children. Let your successes be your confessions to the world. Be a light.

Closing Thoughts

Remember, everything you need to know to let God prosper you is in this book. After you have read this book, don't stop there. Make it a habit to read as little as five minutes a day. The understandings within this book will get into your heart and lead you to success.

The law of "seedtime and harvest" mentioned in this book is a karma-like law God created after the Great Flood. It simply states that whatever you want to receive, you need to plant it as seed by giving it away. Giving *God's Prosperity Promises* a customer review is an excellent way to plant prosperity seeds. You will be helping others to prosper.

I promise you that when you take the time to do good things to others, it will multiply and come back to you. The sooner our brothers and sisters in Christ receive the incredibly helpful information found in this one-of-kind book, the sooner they too can be on the path to increased prosperity. Show your love and care for others by giving a customer review today.

Another Book by Daniel R. Williamson

Trusting Both God and Science
*Reconciling the Bible and Science
Concerning Creation*

Trusting Both God and Science is written by a man who believes God has given him the spirit and power of the Old Testament prophet, Daniel. This book will give the reader an understanding of God's written Word that is in agreement with scientific facts concerning creation. Since God created the universe and everything in it, God created scientific facts as well. Obviously no understanding of God's written Word about how everything began can possibly be correct without its being in agreement with scientific facts. The Bible does not need to be corrected; it is always truthful. It's our understanding of the Bible that needs updating from time to time. If you are searching for a deeper understanding of God's Word, or if you are one of the many Christians who have struggled with reconciling biblical interpretations with evidence of science, this book is a must for you.

Facing the Truth
(Excerpt of Trusting Both God and Science)

The Bible is God's written Word which was spoken to His servants, the prophets of old. Christians consider God's written Word to be the absolute truth.

God also spoke the Word that created the universe and everything within it. In a way, scientific facts are a type of God's written Word to us about how He created the universe. Scientists and science-minded people believe that scientific facts are the absolute truth.

Since God's spoken Word to the prophets and God's spoken Word to nature created both the Bible and scientific facts, it is not logical for them to ever be in disagreement. Scientists don't create scientific facts; God alone creates them. Scientists only discover the facts.

Do you find yourself in disagreement with what I have written? If so, I can give you a good reason for your unbelief. We are human, and humans have subconscious minds. Subconscious minds label all new information as false, or at least suspicious if it is not in agreement with what we already believe.

Scientists also tell us that we believe what we want to believe and that what we want to believe is usually what is in agreement with what we already believe.

So many of us would like to believe we make our decisions based on logic, but the truth is that we usually make decisions based on what we already believe and want to believe.

If you can place aside your beliefs long enough to judge new information with an opened mind, you are truly a very special person, a rare one indeed.

If you are satisfied with your current understanding of God's written Word concerning creation, I'm happy for you, but if you desire deeper knowledge as to how God created everything, I have good news. God has provided His children with all that is needed to reveal the deeper mysteries of creation found in His written Word.

God has provided us with two road maps to lead us to the deeper truths about creation. One road map by itself will never be enough to arrive at the deeper truths of creation.

Our first road map is God's written Word. It must be in agreement with our second road map, which are scientific facts.

God's spoken Word created scientific facts. Scientists trust that scientific facts are true. Since God's spoken Word created scientific facts, how can we as Christians not also trust these facts?

Scientists will never find the truth about the creation of the universe without the Bible, and Christians will never know the true meaning of God's written Word without scientific facts. The Bible and scientific facts are actually two sides of the same coin.

The idea that both God's written Word and scientific facts were created by God's spoken Word and are both a type of written Word that must be read together in order for us to arrive at the truth will be a new concept to many readers.

Since our subconscious minds don't like or trust new ideas that are not in agreement with what we already believe, they will be working overtime trying to convince us to reject these new thoughts. If we are ever to know the truth about how God created everything, we will have to fight our own subconscious minds.

A demonstration as to how to use the two road maps God gave us, in order to arrive at a true understanding of creation, will be useful.

[1] In the beginning God created the heaven and the earth.

^{2} And the earth was without form, and void; and darkness was upon the face of the deep. And the Spirit of God moved upon the face of the waters.
^{3} And God said, Let there be light: and there was light.
^{4} And God saw the light, that it was good: and God divided the light from the darkness.
^{5} And God called the light Day, and the darkness he called Night. And the evening and the morning were the first day.

Genesis 1:1-5

The preceding Bible verses are part of our first road map to find the truth concerning the creation of light created on Creation Day One. We can trust God's written Word to be the absolute truth, but, even so, our first road map doesn't go deep enough to tell the complete story of the creation of light on Creation Day One.

We learn by reading Colossians 1:12, I Timothy 6:16, Acts 26:13, and I John 1:5 that there are many kinds of light mentioned in the Bible. How are we to know for certain what kind of light God actually created, especially since scientists say they know for sure that the first thing created was not light from our sun, or electromagnetic energy?

Because of God's mercy, He has provided His children with a second road map, or scientific facts. Without scientific facts, we would probably never have known that our understanding of God's written Word concerning the creation of light was incomplete.

Before solving any problem, we must know there is a problem. Scientific facts shine a spotlight on problems regarding our understandings of God's written Word. I thank God for the truth, even if the truth means I will need to dig deeper in my understanding of God's written Word. To those who aren't buying what you just read, it could be that you need your hearts pricked. I'm no Apostle Peter, but I will try to get the job done.

The Bible was not removed from our schools because it was false; it was removed because of the false understandings that were being preached about it and the untruths that were being told about scientific knowledge.

There are those who say they cannot be wrong in their beliefs because they have the Holy Spirit to lead them to all truths, but I say to them, "Then why are there so many different opinions and beliefs held by Christians concerning the meaning of God's written Word? Shouldn't we all have the same understandings about the meaning of God's written Word since we all have the same Holy Spirit?"

Truly we all do have the same Holy Spirit to lead us to all truths, but the Holy Spirit is a gentleman. He gently reminds us about what is written in the Bible and gives us helpful suggestions. He doesn't give us orders. If we want the Holy Spirit's help, we will have to humble ourselves by being willing to change our beliefs when needed.

We are no different from those well-meaning, God-loving Christians who were the main cause of the Bible being removed from our schools. They truly believed they were doing the will of God when they were actually preaching their own understandings and beliefs about God's written Word. Some Christians love to blame the scientists and others for the removal of the Bible from the schools; and, in truth, they did do their part in this deed, but the lion's share of the blame falls squarely on the shoulders of those who preached false understandings about the Bible and science.

For the sake of well-educated, scientific-minded youth of today, don't let scientists be the only adults in the room. We need to show our spiritual maturity by being ready to change our minds when the Holy Spirit asks us to.

To the die-hard critics who are still not buying what I am selling, please consider the following. With research, scientists have proven our minds are not usually logical because we normally believe what we want to believe. Also, what we want to believe is usually in agreement with what we already believe.

As a man who took pride in believing I was logical in my decision making and in the things I believed, the above scientific research was very upsetting. I wondered how it could possibly be true, so I searched God's written Word for answers.

Only the Bible has the answer as to why the human mind behaves the way it does and why we are all born with a sin nature. The words Satan used to entice Eve were spirit and power. We can know this is true because Satan is a spirit being and a son of God (Job 1:6).

When Satan spoke to Eve in the Garden of Eden, she received an evil spirit, or a curse. The evil spirit that enticed Eve received power as the result of her imaging that the forbidden fruit was good to eat and that God was wrong about what would happen to them if they ate of it.

Once the evil spirit from Satan received power, it caused Eve to believe what she wanted to believe. Eve's evil spirit is now the source of the sin nature of every human who is born. Sin nature is the ability to believe what we want to believe instead of what is logical. Today, we know Eve's evil spirit received from Satan as the man of sin, or the son of perdition.

[1] Now we beseech you, brethren, by the coming of our Lord Jesus Christ, and by our gathering together unto him,

[2] That ye be not soon shaken in mind, or be troubled, neither by spirit, nor by word, nor by letter as from us, as that the day of Christ is at hand.

[3] Let no man deceive you by any means: for that day shall not come, except there come a falling away first, and that man of sin be revealed, the son of perdition;

[4] Who opposeth and exalteth himself above all that is called God, or that is worshipped; so that he as God sitteth in the temple of God, shewing himself that he is God.

[5] Remember ye not, that, when I was yet with you, I told you these things?

[6] And now ye know what withholdeth that he might be revealed in his time.

[7] For the mystery of iniquity doth already work: only he who now letteth will let, until he be taken out of the way.

[8] And then shall that Wicked be revealed, whom the Lord shall consume with the spirit of his mouth, and shall destroy with the brightness of his coming:

[9] Even him, whose coming is after the working of Satan with all power and signs and lying wonders,

[10] And with all deceivableness of unrighteousness in them that perish; because they received not the love of the truth, that they might be saved.

[11] And for this cause God shall send them strong delusion, that they should believe a lie:

[12] That they all might be damned who believed not the truth, but had pleasure in unrighteousness.

II Thessalonians 2:1-12

The man of sin sits in the temple of God from where he influences our subconscious mind, which in turn influences our conscious mind.

Know ye not that ye are the temple of God, and that the Spirit of God dwelleth in you?

I Corinthians 3:16

Do you realize what we just did? We used scientific knowledge and Bible understanding to arrive at the truth as to why it is so hard for humans to be logical when it comes to deciding what to believe or not to believe.

Knowing why it is so hard to think logically is the key to knowing how to think logically. Knowledge is power.

Fellow Christians, be prepared to be absolutely amazed by all the deep Bible understandings you will receive by using both Bible understandings and scientific knowledge.

available at amazon . com

Trust me, you will love it .

Made in the USA
Monee, IL
29 March 2021